Mighty Machines
Fire Trucks

by Carol K. Lindeen

Consulting Editor: Gail Saunders-Smith, PhD

Capstone
press

Mankato, Minnesota

Pebble Plus is published by Capstone Press,
151 Good Counsel Drive, P.O. Box 669, Mankato, Minnesota 56002.
www.capstonepress.com

1 2 3 4 5 6 10 09 08 07 06 05

Library of Congress Cataloging-in-Publication Data
Lindeen, Carol K., 1976–
    Fire trucks / by Carol K. Lindeen.
    p. cm.—(Pebble plus: mighty machines)
    Includes bibliographical references and index.
    ISBN-13: 978-0-7368-3653-1 (hardcover)
    ISBN-10: 0-7368-3653-5 (hardcover)
    ISBN-13: 978-0-7368-5139-8 (softcover pbk.)
    ISBN-10: 0-7368-5139-9 (softcover pbk.)
    1. Fire engines—Juvenile literature. I. Title. II. Series.
TH9372.T78 2005
628.9'259—dc22   2004020930

Summary: Simple text and photographs present fire trucks, their parts, and how firefighters use fire trucks.

Editorial Credits
Mari C. Schuh, editor; Molly Nei, set designer; Kate Opseth and Ted Williams, book designers;
    Jo Miller, photo researcher; Scott Thoms, photo editor

Photo Credits
Capstone Press/Gary Sundermeyer, cover; Karon Dubke, 14–15
Corbis/George Hall, 7
Folio Inc./David Frazier, 20–21
George Hall Photography LLC/Code Red/Dave Dubowski, 5, 18–19; George Hall, 12–13; John Cetrino, 8–9
Index Stock Imagery/Tom Ross, 11
OneBlueShoe, 1
911 Pictures, 17

Pebble Plus thanks the Mankato Fire Department in Mankato, Minnesota, and members of the Mapleton Fire Department in Mapleton, Minnesota, for their assistance with this book.

Note to Parents and Teachers

The Mighty Machines set supports national standards related to science, technology, and society. This book describes and illustrates fire trucks. The images support early readers in understanding the text. The repetition of words and phrases helps early readers learn new words. This book also introduces early readers to subject-specific vocabulary words, which are defined in the Glossary section. Early readers may need assistance to read some words and to use the Table of Contents, Glossary, Read More, Internet Sites, and Index sections of the book.

Table of Contents

What Are Fire Trucks?

Fire trucks are vehicles
that firefighters use
to put out fires.

STAY BACK 500 FT

M 89 672

Fire Truck Parts

Fire trucks have

flashing lights and sirens.

They warn cars

to get out of the way.

Fire trucks have hoses.
Firefighters hook hoses
to hydrants to get water.

Fire trucks have ladders.
Firefighters climb ladders
to get to fires.

To the Rescue

The alarm rings
at the fire station.

Firefighters get in
the fire trucks.

They rush to the fire.

One firefighter drives
the fire truck.
She sits in the cab.
Other firefighters
ride in the back.

Fire fighters jump
out of the truck.
They pull hoses
out of the truck.

Water flows through
the hose from the hydrant.
Firefighters use tools on their
fire truck to stop the fire.

Firefighters use fire trucks

to help people in emergencies.

Glossary

alarm—a buzzer or bell that gives a warning or signal

cab—the driver's area of a large truck or machine

emergency—something that happens with no warning and requires action right away

fire station—a building where fire trucks are kept; firefighters work and sometimes live at a fire station.

hydrant—a large outdoor pipe connected to a water supply; firefighters use hydrants to help fight fires.

siren—an object that makes a very loud sound as a warning

vehicle—something that carries people or goods from one place to another; fire trucks, ambulances, and police cars are types of vehicles.

Read More

Gordon, Sharon. *What's Inside a Fire Truck?* What's Inside? New York: Benchmark Books, 2004.

Jango-Cohen, Judith. *Fire Trucks.* Pull Ahead Books. Minneapolis: Lerner, 2003.

Miller, Heather. *Fire Trucks.* Wheels, Wings, and Water. Chicago: Heinemann Library, 2003.

Internet Sites

FactHound offers a safe, fun way to find Internet sites related to this book. All of the sites on FactHound have been researched by our staff.

Here's how:

1. Visit *www.facthound.com*

2. Type in this special code **0736836535** for age-appropriate sites. Or enter a search word related to this book for a more general search.

3. Click on the **Fetch It** button.

FactHound will fetch the best sites for you!

Index

Word Count: 127
Grade: 1
Early-Intervention Level: 14